Milwaukee Towne Corporation, Petitioner, v. Loew's Incorporated, a Corporation, et al. U.S. Supreme Court Transcript of Record with Supporting Pleadings

THOMAS C MCCONNELL, MILES G SEELEY, THOMAS C MCCONNELL

Milwaukee Towne Corporation, Petitioner, v. Loew's Incorporated, a Corporation, et al.

Petition / THOMAS C MCCONNELL / 1951 / 439 / 342 U.S. 909 / 72 S.Ct. 302 / 96 L.Ed. 680 / 11-21-1951

Milwaukee Towne Corporation, Petitioner, v. Loew's Incorporated, a Corporation, et al.

Brief in Opposition (P) / MILES G SEELEY / 1951 / 439 / 342 U.S. 909 / 72 S.Ct. 302 / 96 L.Ed. 680 / 12-19-1951

Milwaukee Towne Corporation, Petitioner, v. Loew's Incorporated, a Corporation, et al.

Reply Brief (P) / THOMAS C MCCONNELL / 1951 / 439 / 342 U.S. 909 / 72 S.Ct. 302 / 96 L.Ed. 680 / 1-4-1952

Milwaukee Towne Corporation, Petitioner, v.
Loew's Incorporated, a Corporation, et al. U.S.
Supreme Court Transcript of Record with
Supporting Pleadings

Table of Contents

IN THE

Supreme Court of the United States

OCTOBER TERM, 1951.

No. 439

MILWAUKEE TOWNE CORPORATION, A CORPORATION,
Petitioner,

vs.

LOEW'S INCORPORATED, A CORPORATION; PARA-
MOUNT PICTURES, INC., A CORPORATION; RKO RADIO
PICTURES, INC., A CORPORATION; TWENTIETH CEN-
TURY-FOX FILM CORPORATION, A CORPORATION;
WARNER BROS. PICTURES DISTRIBUTING COR-
PORATION, A CORPORATION; WARNER BROS. CIR-
CUIT MANAGEMENT CORPORATION, A CORPORA-
TION; WARNER BROS. THEATRES, INC., A CORPORA-
TION; AND COLUMBIA PICTURES CORPORATION,
A CORPORATION,

Respondents.

**PETITION FOR A WRIT OF CERTIORARI TO THE
UNITED STATES COURT OF APPEALS FOR
THE SEVENTH CIRCUIT AND BRIEF IN SUP-
PORT THEREOF.**

THOMAS C. McCONNELL,
Attorney for Petitioner.

THE GUNTHORP-WARREN PRINTING COMPANY, 810 WEST JACKSON, CHICAGO

INDEX.

CITATIONS.

Cases.

Statutes and Miscellaneous.

No. ....

MILWAUKEE TOWNE CORPORATION, A CORPORATION,

Petitioner,

vs.

L O E W'S INCORPORATED, A CORPORATION; P A R A-
MOUNT PICTURES, INC., A CORPORATION; RKO RADIO
PICTURES, INC., A CORPORATION; TWENTIETH CEN-
TURY-FOX FILM CORPORATION, A CORPORATION;
WARNER BROS. PICTURES DISTRIBUTING COR-
PORATION, A CORPORATION; WARNER BROS. CIR-
CUIT MANAGEMENT CORPORATION, A CORPORA-
TION; WARNER BROS. THEATRES, INC., A CORPORA-
TION; AND COLUMBIA PICTURES CORPORATION,
A CORPORATION,

Respondents.

PETITION FOR A WRIT OF CERTIORARI.

*To the Honorable the Chief Justice and Associate Justices
of the Supreme Court of the United States:*

Your petitioner, Milwaukee Towne Corporation, a corporation, respectfully prays that a writ of certiorari may
issue to the United States Court of Appeals for the Seventh
Circuit to review its mandate and opinion reversing in
part a judgment of the District Court for $1,295,878.26

plus costs of suit and attorney's fees. The District Court had found respondents guilty of an illegal price-fixing conspiracy and a conspiracy to monopolize the first run exhibition of motion pictures in the City of Milwaukee, Wisconsin, which proximately caused $431,959.42 of damage to petitioner's motion picture theatre business (R. 3349).

JURISDICTION.

The jurisdiction of this Court is invoked under Section 240(a) of the Judicial Code as amended by the Act of February 13, 1925, 43 Stat. 938, 28 U. S. C. A. Sec. 347(a).

The judgment of the Court of Appeals was entered on July 17, 1951 (R. 3751) and respondents' petition for rehearing was denied on September 4, 1951 (R. 3792).

OPINION BELOW.

The opinion of the Court of Appeals appears in the record at page 3751 and is reported in 190 F. (2d) 561. The District Court filed no opinion but its findings and conclusions appear in the record at pages 3326 to 3349.

SUMMARY STATEMENT OF THE MATTER INVOLVED.

Petitioner brought this suit under Sections 1, 2 and 7 of the Sherman Act, 26 Stat. 209-210, and Section 4 of the Clayton Act, 38 Stat. 731, 15 U. S. C. A. Sections 1, 2 and 15, for an injunction and to recover treble damages. The complaint was that respondents maintained a monopoly of first run exhibition of motion pictures in the City of Milwaukee, Wisconsin, which was an integral part of a conspiracy to fix admission prices to motion picture theatres, as a result of which petitioner was prevented from showing motion pictures in a downtown Milwaukee theatre leased by it until after such pictures had been shown in respondents' competing theatres (R. 4-12).

After a trial lasting almost six weeks the District Court entered detailed findings covering every phase of the controversy and found, as the Court of Appeals says in its opinion, "that the defendants were engaged in a conspiracy to monopolize the exhibition of motion pictures and the operation of motion picture theatres in the City of Milwaukee and to restrain trade and commerce in the licensing thereof, and as a result plaintiff was damaged" (R. 3753).

The trial court found petitioner damaged in the amount of $431,959.42 (R. 3349) and entered judgment for $1,295,878.26 and costs (R. 3350). On a subsequent hearing petitioner was allowed the sum of $225,000.00 in reimbursement of its attorney's fees (R. 3625), and a decree of injunction was entered against respondents (R. 3626-3632).

As stated by the Court of Appeals: "Briefly, the record discloses that defendants or their predecessors in 1930 formulated a plan which was revised in 1933, known as the Milwaukee Plan. That this plan amounted to a conspiracy in violation of the anti-trust laws is not seriously disputed. It is plain that under this plan certain theatres, some of which were owned and operated by the defendants, were awarded a first run position for the exhibition of films with certain designated periods of clearances, and that others were awarded a second run position, also with certain designated periods of clearances over subsequent runs. It is shown that the theatre subsequently acquired by plaintiff was designated as a second run theatre, and we think it is reasonable to conclude, as the court found, that it continued to occupy such a position after it was acquired by the plaintiff'' (R. 3755).

Both the District Court (R. 3346) and the Court of Appeals (R. 3755) found that the Milwaukee Plan was illegal and that it damaged petitioner. The latter court held, however, that in the period between May 2, 1946, the date on which petitioner opened its theatre, and August 15, 1946, the date on which the theatre was closed for remodeling, no "fact of damage" was proved because, as the reviewing court said, petitioner had made no demand for first run pictures for that particular period of time.

The trial court had found on conflicting oral testimony that petitioner had made such a demand from all of respondents' companies (Finding 34, R. 3338). The trial court also found that only after the request for first run pictures had been refused and "in order to keep its theatre open" the petitioner "requested and obtained pictures second run" (Finding 35, R. 3338). The reviewing court held that petitioner's witness, Andrew M. Spheeris, a young lawyer and a graduate of the University of Wisconsin and its Law School (R. 362) and a Lieutenant Colonel in the United States Army (R. 363) whose integrity had never been questioned, had not testified truthfully as to the making of these demands. The trial court, however, who had observed the demeanor of the witness under cross-examination had found that he told the truth (R. 3338). The young lawyer is thus condemned a perjurer by a court which never saw him and on opposing testimony which the trial court held came from the mouths of perjurers (R. 3566).

Over and beyond the violence done to the provisions of Rule 52(a) of the Federal Rules of Civil Procedure by this ruling, the reviewing court enunciated the rule that in the absence of a demand for a first run playing position in the illegal system petitioner had no cause of action under the anti-trust laws for damages occasioned by the conspiracy which had assigned petitioner's theatre to an inferior playing position. The proof was conclusive that the conspirators refused to do business with petitioner, even during the period in which the court of review finds that a demand was made, except as a second-run theatre under the Milwaukee Plan (R. 370, 374, 375, 520, 521, 365, 371, 373, 468, 666, 1193). The proof was conclusive that the playing position offered petitioner was the only feasible and possible method by which it could engage in the motion picture business in the presence of this conspiracy in Milwaukee (R. 369-375, 466, 467, 380-381, 666, 520-521; Pltf.'s Exs. 1, 7, 8, 9, 14 and 19, R. 2065, 2093, 2102, 2105, 2112, 2124).

Since the illegal system had wholly monopolized the Milwaukee district for twenty years, nothing could have been more futile than a demand for a first-run playing position as against the theatres owned and operated by respondents. However, the decision of the court of review holds that, no matter how futile, a demand for a first-run playing position under the illegal system was a condition precedent to the bringing of a cause of action for damages, and in the absence of such a demand the "fact of damage," so-called, could not be proved (R. 3761).

In holding that there was no "fact of damage" proved on the present record for the period above mentioned the Court of Appeals in effect has overruled the decision of this Court in the case of *Bigelow, et al.* v. *RKO Radio Pictures, Inc., et al.*, 327 U. S. 251; 90 L. Ed. 652, which held that "the establishment of the discriminatory release system was damaging to the petitioners who were relegated by it to a playing position inferior to that of their competitors."

In holding that such a discriminatory release system is not actionable in the absence of a demand for first run pictures, the reviewing court has by interpolation read into the statutes known as the anti-trust laws an anomalous doctrine to the effect that a tort-feasor commits no tort unless and until his victim complains in writing and demands a cessation of the tort. On this record it has held that no damages can be recovered on account of clearance which the trial court held to be created by conspiracy and thus illegal (Finding 56, R. 3343) in the absence of affirmative proof that the clearance was unreasonable (R. 3362). This Court affirmed the decree in *U. S.* v. *Paramount Pictures, Inc., et al.,* 334 U. S. 131, stating: "Whenever any clearance provision is attacked as not legal under the provisions of this decree, the burden shall be upon the distributor to sustain the legality thereof." The respondents have admitted there is proof in the record of damage occasioned petitioner by the illegal clearance (R. 3352).

The public interest involved in the decision of this question is manifest and apparent because as stated in the case of *Ring* v. *Spina,* 148 F. 2d 647, 653, "* * * plaintiff is precisely the type of individual whom the Sherman Act seeks to protect from combinations fashioned by others and offered to such individual as the only feasible method by which he may do business."

The Court of Appeals also held (R. 3768) that the District Court had abused its discretion in enjoining the cross-licensing of pictures in respondents' theatres by respondent distributors where such theatres had been used to boycott distributors who sold first run pictures to petitioner (Finding 55, R. 3342; R. 271-273, 351, 419, 663, 1793-1794; Pltf.'s Exs. 34-36; R. 2178-2182) as a means of preventing the showing of first run pictures by petitioner's theatre (R. 2178-2182). Here again is presented a question of large importance in the administration of the anti-trust laws.

QUESTIONS PRESENTED.

(1) Do the anti-trust laws grant immunity from a treble damage suit brought by petitioner who according to the reviewing court has made no formal demand for a cessation of the conspiracy where

(a) Respondents have maintained an illegal conspiracy for the releasing of pictures for a period of twenty years and have offered it to petitioner as the only feasible method by which petitioner may do business, and where

(b) Petitioner proved and the trial court found (Finding 56, R. 3343) that in the absence of such conspiracy petitioner would have obtained receipts at least as great as those obtained by respondent's Wisconsin Theatre?

(2) Do the anti-trust laws preclude the issuance of an injunction against cross-licensing by respondents in their own theatres where such theatres have been used as instrumentalities in carrying on a secondary boycott against petitioner's theatre in order to enforce the conspiracy?

REASONS FOR GRANTING THE WRIT.

The discretionary power of this Court to grant a writ of certiorari is invoked upon the following grounds:

1. The Court of Appeals held that the fact of damage in a treble damage suit cannot be shown in the absence of a demand for first run pictures even though a conspiracy which had been found to exist by the reviewing court by its very terms rendered such demand completely futile. This decision is in direct conflict with the decision of this Court in the case of *Bigelow, et al.* v. *RKO Radio Pictures, Inc., et al.*, 327 U. S. 251; 90 L. Ed. 652.

2. The substitution by the Court of Appeals of its own inferences and conclusions for those of the District Court on the question of the credibility of petitioner's witness who testified that a demand for first run pictures had been made does violence to Rule 52(a) of the Federal Rules of Civil Procedure and is in direct conflict with the decision of this Court in the case of *United States* v. *Yellow Cab Co.*, 338 U. S. 338; 94 L. Ed. 150.

3. The Court of Appeals has decided important questions of Federal law in a manner which in effect deprives the public of the benefit of civil suits under the anti-trust laws and tends to discourage the bringing of such suits and to encourage the violation of these laws. The consequent injury to the public is so direct and manifest as to call for the exercise of this Court's power of supervision.

Wherefore, it is respectfully submitted that this petition for a writ of certiorari to the Court of Appeals for the Seventh Circuit should be granted.

Respectfully submitted,

MILWAUKEE TOWNE CORPORATION,

By THOMAS C. McCONNELL,

Attorney for Petitioner.

IN THE

Supreme Court of the United States

OCTOBER TERM, 1951.

No.

MILWAUKEE TOWNE CORPORATION, A CORPORATION,
Petitioner,

vs.

L O E W'S INCORPORATED, A CORPORATION; P A R A-
MOUNT PICTURES, INC., A CORPORATION; RKO RADIO
PICTURES, INC., A CORPORATION; TWENTIETH CEN-
TURY-FOX FILM CORPORATION, A CORPORATION;
WARNER BROS. PICTURES DISTRIBUTING COR-
PORATION, A CORPORATION; WARNER BROS. CIR-
CUIT MANAGEMENT CORPORATION, A CORPORA-
TION; WARNER BROS. THEATRES, INC., A CORPORA-
TION; AND COLUMBIA PICTURES CORPORATION,
A CORPORATION,

Respondents.

BRIEF IN SUPPORT OF PETITION FOR A WRIT OF CERTIORARI.

STATEMENT OF THE CASE.

The essential facts of the case are stated in the accompanying petition for a writ of certiorari.

JURISDICTION.

The jurisdiction of this Court is shown in the accompanying petition.

OPINION BELOW.

The opinion of the Court of Appeals is found at page 3751 of the record and is reported in 190 F. (2d) 561.

SPECIFICATION OF ERRORS.

If a writ of certiorari is issued, petitioner intends to urge that the Court of Appeals for the Seventh Circuit erred:

(1) In setting aside the trial court's findings of petitioner's damages in the amount of $118,101.32, being the damages for the period between May 2, 1946 and August 15, 1946.

(2) In setting aside the trial court's findings as to the amount of petitioner's reasonable attorney's fees to be awarded as part of the costs of suit.

(3) In vacating that part of the District Court's injunction decree which prohibited the cross-licensing by respondents of motion pictures in their theatres so long as such theatres were owned, leased or operated by respondents or their subsidiary companies.

ARGUMENT.

I.

The Court of Appeals Has By Judicial Interpolation Deprived Most Litigants and the Public of the Benefit of Treble Damage Suits in the Seventh Circuit.

The District Court (R. 3347) and the Court of Appeals (R. 3755) both found that the discriminatory system of release which caused petitioner's damage was illegal. The latter Court held:

"Briefly, the record discloses that defendants or their predecessors in 1930 formulated a plan which was revised in 1933, known as the Milwaukee Plan. That this plan amounted to a conspiracy in violation of the anti-trust laws is not seriously disputed. It is plain that under this plan certain theatres, some of which were owned and operated by the defendants, were awarded a first run position for the exhibition of films with certain designated periods of clearances, and that others were awarded a second run position, also with certain designated periods of clearances over subsequent runs. It is shown that the theatre subsequently acquired by plaintiff was designated as a second run theatre, * * *" (R. 3755).

The reviewing court then held that in the period from May 2, 1946, when petitioner first opened its theatre for business, and August 15, 1946, when the theatre was closed for remodeling—(a period which the Court designated as the "first damage period") petitioner could recover no damages because the "fact of damage" was not shown (R. 3758). To reach this position the Court of Appeals first had to set aside the trial court's findings, based on controverted oral testimony, that a demand for a first run playing position had been made by petitioner during the period in question (Finding 34, R. 3338) and had been refused because the illegal system classified petitioner's theatre in a second run playing position. After thus doing violence to the provisions of Rule 52(a) of the Federal Rules of Civil Procedure the Court of Appeals went further to hold as a matter of law that "* * * it cannot be held that defendants' conspiracy was the direct and proximate cause of plaintiffs' damage because it was prevented from negotiating and obtaining first run pictures *in the absence of a demand or request*" (R. 3761) (Italics ours).

The question thus posed by this petition is a pure question of law as to whether or not a plaintiff, opposed by an illegal conspiracy to monopolize the first run exhibition of motion picture films, must make an absolutely futile demand as a condition precedent to maintaining an action for damages under the anti-trust laws. That the demand would have been futile is conclusively shown by the fact that the Court of Appeals found that such a demand had been made after the remodeling of the theatre and had been refused by respondents because of the illegal system of release which precluded petitioner's theatre from a first run playing position (Rec. 3758).

It is clear, as stated by this Court in *Bigelow, et al.* v. *RKO Radio Pictures, Inc., et al.,* 327 U. S. 251, 262; 90 L. Ed. 652, 659, that petitioner was "entitled, as of right, to continue to purchase and show films which had not had prior showing free of the restraints of the unlawful distribution system."

It should be obvious that the deprivation of a right of this kind by conspiracy is actionable without going through the futile act of demanding that the conspiracy cease. As stated in *William Goldman Theatres, Inc.,* v. *Loew's, Inc., et al.,* 150 F. (2d) 738, 744:

> "* * * a course of conduct, by those who own all of the other available theatres in that area, and those who distribute the product, which eliminates from competition the owner of the available theatre, constitutes a violation of the statute."

That proof of a discriminatory release system founded in conspiracy establishes the fact of damage as a matter of law is shown by the decision of this Court in *Bigelow, et al.* v. *RKO Radio Pictures, Inc., et al.*, 327 U. S. 251, 260; 90 L. Ed. 652, 658:

> "Upon the record in this case it is indisputable that the jury could have found that during the period in question a first or prior run theatre possessed competitive advantages over later run theatres, because of its greater capacity to attract patronage to pictures which had not been shown elsewhere, and its ability to charge higher admission prices than subsequent run theatres, and that, other things being equal, the establishment of the discriminatory release system was damaging to the petitioners who were relegated by it to a playing position inferior to that of their competitors."

On the present record there is no question as to whether or not the discriminatory release system relegated petitioner to a playing position inferior to that of its competitors, to its damage. The purpose of the conspiracy was to maintain a monopoly of first run exhibition in respondents' theatres (R. 268, 269). Obviously, if the conspiracy did not have this effect there was no point to the conspiracy. That fact was admitted by respondents' own witnesses. Perlewitz, one of the participants in the conspiracy, testified that the Milwaukee Plan was designed to prevent petitioner's theatre from playing first run and accomplished that result (R. 210); Ruby, a respondents' witness, said that he was not free to sell petitioner's theatre anything but second run under the Plan (R. 1647); Fitzgerald, the manager of the Fox theatres in Milwaukee, testified that petitioner's theatre was classified as a second run theatre under the Plan (R. 245) and that the provisions of the Plan were incorporated into his company's contracts with all the distributors down to the date of the lawsuit (R. 246). Respondents themselves admitted that prior run theatres possessed competitive advantages over later run theatres because of the former's greater capacity to attract patronage to pictures which had not been shown elsewhere and their ability to charge higher admission prices than subsequent run theatres (R. 359, 659, 660-662, 678, 1032, 1166, 1241-1244, 1394, 1479, 1488, 1635). Respondents themselves conceded that the "fact of damage" was established by the evidence as to the first damage period and they took issue only as to the amount of such damage.

In the trial court in their objections to the findings respondents stated (R. 3352):

"On the record of this case as it now stands, the best evidence as to the plaintiff's measure of damages for the period from May 2, 1946 to August 15, 1946, during which period the court has found the plaintiff was damaged as a result of illegal clearance granted to first run theatres in the City of Milwaukee, is the difference between the admissions of plaintiff's theatre adjusted for film rental and advertising and the admissions, similarly adjusted, obtained by the Strand Theatre which played on a run immediately after the close of the first run in Milwaukee, which damages would amount to the sum of $41,341.15 as disclosed by Fox's Exhibit 66."

This leaves no support whatever for the position taken by the Court of Appeals that there is no evidence whatever in the record of any fact of damage for the first damage period, except its own erroneous statement that damages occasioned by the illegal system of release cannot be proved "in the absence of a demand or request" (R. 3761).

The trial court found that the fact of damage for the first period did exist (Finding 51, R. 3341; Conclusion 9, R. 3347). The reviewing court said:

"* * * It is shown that the theatre subsequently acquired by plaintiff was designated as a second run theatre, and we think it is reasonable to conclude, as the court found, that it continued to occupy such a position after it was acquired by the plaintiff.'' (R. 3755.)

As we have pointed out, the reviewing court, contrary to the decision of this Court in the *Bigelow* case, *supra,* has held that the "fact of damage" cannot be proved in the absence of a demand for an earlier playing position even though the acceptance of such a demand was precluded by the terms of the very conspiracy which the Court of Appeals found to exist. The reviewing court's decision thus by interpolation reads something into the anti-trust laws that is not there and which is apparently designed to defeat any anti-trust cases in which plaintiff is forced to accept the playing position offered as a condition to staying in business at all.

II.

The Writ of Certiorari Should Issue in Order to Preserve to the Public the Benefits Created By the Treble Damage Provisions of the Anti-Trust Laws.

The reviewing court's manifest hostility to civil anti-trust cases is shown on the face of its opinion when it states:

"It would be almost an impossible task to go through this voluminous record and even to mention, much less discuss, the many points and circumstances relied upon by plaintiff's counsel in support of the court's findings of conspiracy or by defendants' counsel in an attempted demonstration that such findings are without support, *and the futility of so doing is shown by our previous efforts in this respect, all of which have come to naught.* Our most recent experience was *Kiefer-Stewart Co. v. Joseph E. Seagram & Sons, Inc., et al.,* in which this court (182 F. 2d 228), in a suit for damages under the Sherman Act, thought and held that there was no competent evidence to support a jury finding of the conspiracy alleged. The Supreme Court (340 U. S. 211) in a unanimous opinion and in

> a single paragraph directed at this issue held that the
> evidence was sufficient. And with all due deference to
> the Supreme Court, if there was any evidence to sup-
> port a finding of conspiracy in that case, it is difficult
> to visualize a case where it would not be sufficient.''
> (R. 3754.) (Italics ours.)

This antipathy is further evidenced by the Court's ref-
erence to "* * * the possibility that the anti-trust
laws might develop into a racketeering practice * * *"
(R. 3764). This comment carries the obvious implication
that the reviewing court thinks that a plaintiff and its
attorney who succeed in breaking up by court proceedings
a vicious monopoly and conspiracy, which has throttled
an entire industry in Milwaukee for twenty years, are engaged in some sort of reprehensible activity.

Further, the Court of Appeals for the Seventh Circuit is
notorious for its reversal of plaintiffs' verdicts in civil
suits under the anti-trust laws. In the *Bigelow* case,
supra, it held that no fact of damage was shown on a record that to this Court showed self-evident damage. A
long list of cases could be cited which evidence beyond
peradventure the hostility of the Court of Appeals for
the Seventh Circuit to this type of litigation. Cf. *Mer-
coid Corp.* v. *Minneapolis-Honeywell Reg. Co.*, 133 F. 2d
811; rev'd 320 U. S. 661; *Bigelow* v. *RKO Radio Pictures*,
150 F. 2d 877, rev'd 327 U. S. 251; *Emich Motors* v. *General Motors*, 181 F. 2d 70, rev'd in part 340 U. S. 558;
Kiefer-Stewart Co. v. *Seagram*, 182 F. 2d 228, rev'd 340
U. S. 211.

In the instant case the Court not only dealt the anti-trust
laws a body blow by in effect overruling this Court's decisions on damages thereunder but the Court also attempted
to discourage the prosecution of these cases by interfering
with and reversing the trial court's findings that plaintiff should be entitled to be reimbursed for substantially

all of the attorney's fees which it was required by contract
to pay its attorney and by reversing that part of the injunction decree which represented the trial court's effort
to deal realistically with the use of subsequent run theatres
in carrying on a secondary boycott of petitioner's theatre
and which theatres were used as active implements in the
conspiracy against petitioner's business (Finding 55, R.
3342).

For reasons of very large and important public interest, with which this Court is thoroughly familiar, the supervisory powers of this Court should be exercised in the
instant case if the effectiveness of the anti-trust laws in
breaking up monopoly is to be preserved in the Seventh
Circuit.

Even in cases where a demand creates the right upon
which a suit is predicated, courts have universally held
that such a demand is excused wherever it is shown to be
futile. See *Jefferson Tracey* v. *Mary Irwin, et al.*, 18
Wall. 549, 21 L. Ed. 786 (1873); *Union Naval Stores Company* v. *U. S.*, 240 U. S. 284, 60 L. Ed. 644 (1916).

In conspiracy cases where the right is established by
statute and its invasion prohibited by law, the instant case
is the first to hold that a futile demand is a condition precedent to the recovery of treble damages. Cf. *Straus* v.
Victor Talking Machine.Co., 297 Fed. 791 (3 Cir., 1924);
American Tobacco Co. v. *People's Tobacco Co.*, 204 Fed.
58 (5 Cir., 1913).

Conclusion.

The ruling of the Court of Appeals for the Seventh Circuit in the case at bar is manifestly erroneous and against
public policy and in effect is a reversal of the decisions
of this Court on the same subject matter. The questions
presented are of paramount public importance in the en-
forcement and administration of the anti-trust laws. As

pointed out, the decision of the reviewing court is in direct conflict with the decisions of this and other Federal courts of review.

A decision by the Senior Judge of the District Court in Chicago, vindicating large public interests in the City of Milwaukee, Wisconsin, has been ruthlessly cut to pieces by the imposition of an arbitrary rule of damages which threatens to destroy and defeat the precedent value of this Court's opinion in the *Bigelow* case.

Apparently, unless the supervisory powers of this Court can be invoked, all anti-trust suit plaintiffs are to be made the victims of the repeated attempts of the Court of Appeals for the Seventh Circuit by judicial interpolation to undermine and destroy any effective application of the anti-trust laws in breaking up monopolies and widespread restraints of trade in the ending of which the public has a manifest and vital interest.

It is, therefore, respectfully urged that this Court's supervisory powers should be exercised and that this petition for a writ of certiorari should be granted.

Respectfully submitted,

THOMAS C. McCONNELL,
Attorney for Petitioner.

In the

Supreme Court of the United States

October Term, 1951

No. 439

MILWAUKEE TOWNE CORPORATION,
a corporation,

Petitioner,

vs.

LOEW'S INCORPORATED, a corporation; PARAMOUNT
PICTURES, INC., a corporation; RKO RADIO PIC-
TURES, INC., a corporation; TWENTIETH CENTURY-
FOX FILM CORPORATION, a corporation; WARNER
BROS. PICTURES DISTRIBUTING CORPORATION,
a corporation; WARNER BROS. CIRCUIT MANAGE-
MENT CORPORATION, a corporation; WARNER
BROS. THEATRES, INC., a corporation; and COLUM-
BIA PICTURES CORPORATION, a corporation,

Respondents.

On Petition for a Writ of Certiorari to the United
States Court of Appeals for the Seventh Circuit

BRIEF FOR THE RESPONDENTS IN OPPOSITION

Miles G. Seeley
Edward R. Johnston
John F. Caskey
Vincent O'Brien
Attorneys for the Respondents

December 18, 1951.

TABLE OF CONTENTS

TABLE OF CASES

Milwaukee Towne Corporation,
a corporation,

> Petitioner,

vs.

Loew's Incorporated, a corporation; Paramount Pictures, Inc., a corporation; RKO Radio Pictures, Inc., a corporation; Twentieth Century-Fox Film Corporation, a corporation; Warner Bros. Pictures Distributing Corporation, a corporation; Warner Bros. Circuit Management Corporation, a corporation; Warner Bros. Theatres, Inc., a corporation; and Columbia Pictures Corporation, a corporation,

> Respondents.

No. 439

On Petition for a Writ of Certiorari to the United States Court of Appeals for the Seventh Circuit

BRIEF FOR THE RESPONDENTS IN OPPOSITION

OPINIONS BELOW

The opinion of the Court of Appeals for the Seventh Circuit is reported in 190 F. 2d 561 (R. 3751). The District Court filed no opinion.

JURISDICTION

The petitioner states that it invokes the jurisdiction of this Court "under Section 240(a) of the Judicial Code as amended by the Act of February 13, 1925. 43 Stat. 938, 28 U.S.C.A. Sec. 347(a)."

STATEMENT

Plaintiff's petition for certiorari advances three reasons for granting the writ (p. 8). The first is that the court below held that the "fact of damage" cannot be established in a treble damage suit under the antitrust laws without a formal demand by the plaintiff for a cessation of the restraint complained of, even when such a demand would be completely futile. That holding is said to conflict with the decision of this Court in *Bigelow* v. *RKO Radio Pictures*, 327 U. S. 251.

This asserted ground for granting the writ presents a false issue. Neither the trial court nor the court below treated this as a case in which no demand had been made because the claimed conspiracy would have rendered such a demand futile. The trial court treated it as a case in which a demand was made and was refused. The court below did treat it as a case in which no demand was made,—but recognized that the reason why there was no demand was that plaintiff knew its theatre was wholly unsuitable for the exhibition of pictures on first run.

Plaintiff's second reason for granting the writ is that the court below did violence to Rule 52(a) of the Federal Rules of Civil Procedure by rejecting findings of the trial court because it was convinced that the testimony on which those findings had been based was perjured. Plaintiff's petition asserts that this was in conflict with *United States* v. *Yellow Cab Co.*, 338 U. S. 338. No such conflict exists.

The final reason asserted by plaintiff for granting the writ is that the court below not only erred, but seriously undermined the antitrust laws, by reducing the trial court's allowance for attorney's fees and striking from the trial court's decree a provision which plaintiff describes as a "ban on cross-licensing", but which actually was a requirement of theatre divestiture by the affiliated exhibitors.

The facts show that the court below committed no error in these respects.

PLAINTIFF'S PETITION MISSTATES THE HOLDING OF THE COURT BELOW WITH RESPECT TO PLAINTIFF'S FAILURE TO PROVE THE FACT OF DAMAGE DURING THE FIRST DAMAGE PERIOD.

Plaintiff's petition (p. 8) would have this Court believe that the court below set aside the award of damages for the "first damage period" solely upon the ground that plaintiff made no demand during that period for pictures to exhibit on first run. Plaintiff asserts that there is presented a "pure question of law" (p.12), thereby suggesting that there is no need for this Court to review the factual basis for the Court of Appeals' decision. It is submitted, however, that a brief review of the factual context of the decision will demonstrate that the question of law which plaintiff's petition seeks to pose is not presented in this record.

What the Court of Appeals actually held was that the plaintiff was not entitled to recover damages for the "first damage period" because (1) it failed to ask for first run pictures because it recognized that it did not then have a theatre suitable for their exhibition and (2) even if plaintiff had then demanded pictures for exhibition on first run, the unsuitability of its theatre would have precluded it from recovering damages for that period.

Plaintiff, during the so-called "first damage period", wanted only second run pictures from the defendants, demanded nothing but second run pictures from them and received exactly what it wanted and demanded. Plaintiff attempted to prove that it had demanded pictures to exhibit on first run during the "first damage period". The trial court found that there had been such a demand, but the court below found, with more than ample justification, that the testimony upon which the trial court's finding was based was perjury (R. 3759).

On April 17, 1946, plaintiff acquired its lease of the old Miller Theatre in Milwaukee (R. 459), which then was being operated by Fox-Wisconsin on second run under a lease expiring April 30, 1946. On the same day plaintiff sent to each of the defendant distributors a formal demand, on the letterhead of **its attorney,** as follows (R. 377-78, 465):

"April 17, 1946

"Gentlemen:

"This is to inform you that Miller Theatre Corp., duly organized under the laws of the State of Wisconsin, will be the lessee of the present Miller Theatre as of May 1, 1946.

"The Miller Theatre Corp. expects to contract for pictures from your company to play as soon as 'second run City of Milwaukee' permits. The recent contractual policy of this theatre will be continued by the newly organized Miller Theatre Corp.

Very truly yours,

Miller Theatre Corp.,
By A. M. Spheeris, President."*

---

*Miller Theatre Corp. was the plaintiff, which subsequently changed its name to Milwaukee Towne Corporation.

Each of the defendant distributors complied promptly and fully with the foregoing demand (R. 1180-81, 1506, 1644-45, 1723-24) and served plaintiff pictures to exhibit on second run from May 1, 1946 until plaintiff closed the Miller Theatre for remodeling on August 15, 1946 (R. 402). That is the period of fifteen weeks referred to in this case as the "first damage period", for which plaintiff claimed and was awarded treble damages amounting to $354,303.96.

Plaintiff's witness Spheeris testified that prior to making the foregoing formal written demand on April 17, 1946, he and Constantine Papas, his associate in organizing plaintiff, together orally requested each of the defendant distributors to license first run pictures for exhibition at the Miller Theatre (R. 369-75).

The supposed oral demands to which Spheeris testified were denied by the Milwaukee branch manager of each of the distributors to whom they were claimed to have been made (R. 724, 1180-81, 1456, 1507-08, 1644-45, 1659, 1724). In addition to that direct refutation, a host of circumstances betrayed the falsity of Spheeris' testimony.

Papas, although present in the courtroom throughout the trial, failed to take the witness stand to corroborate his associate or to refute the testimony of the branch managers.

At the time of their claimed oral demands, Spheeris and Papas did not even have the Miller Theatre under lease. The letter of April 17, 1946 shows upon its face that one of its purposes was to inform the distributors that the plaintiff was going to take over the Miller Theatre. That would have been unnecessary if Spheeris and Papas already had demanded pictures for the Miller Theatre. Moreover, it is incredible that the letter of April 17, 1946, would not have mentioned plaintiffs desire to license first run pictures, if in truth plaintiff then had any such desire.

Plaintiff made in writing not only its demand for second run pictures on April 17, 1946, but also the demands which it made for first run pictures one year and two years later, respectively (Pl. Exs. 77, 169, R. 411, 916, 2333-34, 2428). All of those written demands were reflected in interoffice communications found in the files of the defendants and of the plaintiff but not one scrap of written evidence was produced which referred to any demand in 1946 by the plaintiff upon the defendants for first run pictures (Loew's Ex. 33, R. 3087, 1153-54; Par. Exs. 17, 17A, 19, R. 3195, 3196, 3199, 991-2, 994-95; RKO Exs. 8-12A, R. 3241-45, 1105-07, 1110; Pl. Ex. 277, R. 2717, 915, 683, 989, 1105, 1140, 1181, 1359, 1594, 1655).

Harold Wirthwein, who negotiated the lease between one Rothman, the owner of the Miller Theatre, and Spheeris and Papas and who was to have had a 50% interest in the lease, testified emphatically that it was their intention at the time to operate the Miller as a second run theatre, that the Miller Theatre was not suitable for first run pictures in its then rundown condition and that the percentage rental called for by the lease would have been prohibitive if applied to first run receipts (R. 705, 711-12, 725-26). Neither Papas nor Rothman was called to contradict Wirthwein's testimony.

The president of United Artists, which not only is not a defendant in this case, but is a large stockholder in plaintiff corporation and therefore is heavily interested in the judgment recovered below, testified that on April 18, 1946, Papas and Spheeris told him that they were thinking of a second or third run policy for the Miller Theater and were not ready to discuss the possibility of playing United Artists' pictures on first run (R. 807, 821, 825).

On April 30, 1946, negotiations started between United Artists and plaintiff which resulted in agreements that United Artists would invest money in the plaintiff, that the Miller Theatre would be extensively remodeled and renamed, that a ceiling on the percentage rental would be negotiated and that thereafter plaintiff's theatre would be reopened as the exclusive first run outlet in Milwaukee for United Artists' pictures (R. 808-18).

The Miller Theatre was closed for alterations on August 15, 1946 (R. 402). When it was reopened as the Towne Theatre on December 26, 1946, after an expenditure of nearly $200,000 (R. 406) it was completely changed, even as to name. In the new Towne theatre plaintiff played United Artists' pictures exclusively until June of 1947 (R. 474), when it wrote to some of the defendant distributors, saying:

> "*We are now desirous* of negotiating with you for first run product in the City of Milwaukee." (Pl. Ex. 77, R. 2333-34, 411.) (Emphasis supplied.)

These uncontradicted circumstances are consistent only with the conclusion that plaintiff had no idea of operating a first run theatre until United Artists, which at that time had no satisfactory first run outlet in Milwaukee (R. 818, 852), worked out with it what was in effect a partnership and franchise to change the character and name of the theatre entirely and to use it as an exclusive showcase for the pictures of that distributor. Not until the accumulated backlog of United Artists' pictures had been played off did plaintiff need or want first run pictures from any other distributors.

The real question presented on the record here and decided by the court below was not whether a plaintiff must make a futile demand as a condition precedent to the right to recover treble damages. It was whether this plaintiff had any right to recover treble damages for the "first damage period" because it did not then get from defendant distributors first run pictures which it did not want, did not ask for and was in no position to use profitably at that time.

If there appears from the record any futility about the idea of plaintiff making a demand for first run pictures in April, 1946, it is the futility which plaintiff must have realized arose from the utter unsuitability of the Miller Theatre for the exhibition of such pictures. The president of United Artists testified, without contradiction and with abundant documentary corroboration, that on April 30, 1946 he told Papas and Spheeris that United Artists could not permit its pictures to play on first run in the Miller Theatre until a minimum of $90,000 to $100,000 had been expended to remodel it, its name had been changed to get away from its previous unsavory reputation, and plaintiff's lease had been amended to place a ceiling on its percentage rental (R. 809, 811).*

————

*Edward C. Raftery, the President of United Artists, which is not a defendant here but is a one-third owner of the plaintiff corporation, testified:

"Well, I told Mr. Papas and Mr. Spheeris that in my opinion, before that theatre was fit for the exhibition of first run pictures, there would have to be a substantial amount of money spent. I said, 'First of all, you need new chairs throughout the whole house. It needs to be completely redecorated. You need entire new plumbing. It looks like a new electrical job complete. You have got to do new carpeting, you need to redo the lobby, build a new marquee,' and Mr. Papas volunteered the information, or Mr. Spheeris, I don't know which, that the theatre had a bad reputation in the town, that people wouldn't want to send their children to the theatre.

"I said, 'Well, if that is the case, the first thing that ought to be done is change the name of the theatre, and get new signs, start it all over from scratch, because,' I said, 'many years ago I found out the Miller Theatre was considered a good vaudeville theatre in Milwaukee.'

"They asked me what I thought would have to be spent. 'Well,' I said, 'I don't see how you can do any kind of a job here unless you spend somewhere around ninety to a hundred

As the court below noted in its opinion, not even the findings of the trial court, although they were drafted by plaintiff's counsel, contained a finding that plaintiff's theatre was
suitable for the exhibition of first run pictures prior to December 26, 1946 but, on the contrary, such findings recognized by
implication that the old Miller Theatre was not suitable for
that purpose (R. 3760).

After December 26, 1946, plaintiff had what was really a
new theatre, the Towne Theatre, suitable for first run pictures.
Thereafter, plaintiff admittedly made demands for first run pictures but the results of its demands did not indicate that they
were futile. All eight of the "major distributors" are claimed to
have been parties to a conspiracy dating back to 1933 to prevent
the Miller Theatre from becoming a first run house. Yet, before plaintiff brought or threatened the present action, five of
those eight distributors had acted in a manner irreconcilable
with the claimed conspiracy. United Artists not only licensed
plaintiff but gave it a virtual franchise and helped it to remodel
its theatre in 1946 (Pl. Ex. 79 B, R. 2342, 546). In 1947,
Universal licensed many first run pictures to plaintiff (R. 410,
503-04) and Columbia negotiated with plaintiff (R. 1594-
1606) but the parties did not agree on terms. In 1948, prior

---

thousand dollars; and at that, all you'll do is re-seat it, re-carpet,
change the sides where those—toward the screen; new boothing
equipment, new sound, new marquee'; and I also made the
suggestion they ought to try to rent that store next to the lobby
and put a nice ladies' rest room in there, because the one in the
cellar and in the mezzanine were—they were terrible; they were
so small and inadequate, and I said, 'You can't make any struc-
tural changes for that figure. And,' I said, 'with costs going up
the way they are, the chances are you may run above that figure.'" (R. 809)

Raftery made a contemporaneous memorandum of his recommenda-
tions for making the Miller Theatre suitable for first run pictures,
which is in evidence as Loew's Exhibit 11 (R. 3033).

to the institution of this action, Loew's and Paramount each offered plaintiff competitive bidding for its pictures on first run (Loew's Ex. 142, R. 3118, 1873; Par. Ex. 10, R. 3154, 997).

Plaintiff's only demands which remained in the "futile" category, to the extent that they had not been complied with, were those it had made of Twentieth-Century Fox and Warner, each of which had its own affiliated first run theatres in Milwaukee (Fox Ex 59, R. 3003, 1751, 1193) and upon RKO, which decided to license its pictures to an independent competitor of plaintiff which had no other first run major product (R. 1107-09).

Plaintiff nevertheless was permitted to recover $941,-574.30 treble damages for that period—December 26, 1946 to July 20, 1948. The errors of law involved in that award are the subject of a petition for certiorari by the defendants herein (No. 454).

It is submitted that the court below was entirely correct in ruling, upon the record before it, that plaintiff's failure in 1946 to ask for first run pictures for the old Miller Theatre, or for anything else which it did not get from the defendants, precluded it from recovering any damages for the period from May 1 to August 15, 1946.

Moreover, the unsuitability of the old Miller Theatre for the profitable exhibition of pictures on first run would compel a finding that the plaintiff was not damaged during the "first damage period" herein, even if the trial court's holding that it demanded pictures for first run during that period could be sustained. The court below did not think that it reached that question, because it found that no demands had been made. Nevertheless, it indicated clearly how it would resolve that question when it said:

> "* * * Moreover, plaintiff claims no damage for the period from August 15, 1946 to December 26,

1946 (the period when plaintiff's theatre was closed for remodeling). If plaintiff's theory is tenable, that it is entitled to recovery merely upon a showing of a conspiracy by the defendants to relegate its theatre to one of a second run position, it would be logical to expect that damages would have been claimed for that period. Obviously, no damages were claimed for that period because plaintiff was not in a position to use first run pictures, and we think by the same token it was not entitled to recover damages for the preceding period because *not only did it fail to make a demand or request for first run pictures but recognized that its theatre was not suitable for that purpose.*"   (R. 3761-62, Emphasis supplied.)

Even if this Court were to grant certiorari herein on plaintiff's petition and even if it were to find that the court below erred both as to the necessity of a demand and as to whether any demand was made, it still could not properly reverse the judgment below unless it were prepared to find affirmatively, in the absence of any such finding by the trial court and in the face of the contrary opinion of the court below, that plaintiff's theatre was suitable for the profitable exhibition of first run pictures during the first damage period.

THE DECISION BELOW, WITH RESPECT TO THE "FACT OF DAMAGE" POINT, IS NOT IN CONFLICT WITH THIS COURT'S DECISION IN *BIGELOW* v. *RKO RADIO PICTURES.*

In *Bigelow* v. *RKO Radio Pictures*, 327 U. S. 251; no question was decided about the necessity of a "futile" demand. The plaintiffs in that case had made frequent but unavailing demands on all of the major distributors to move up their theatre from fourth neighborhood run to third neighborhood run.

This Court did not hold in the *Bigelow* case, as plaintiff's petition contends, that proof of an alleged system of release, without more, is sufficient to establish the "fact of damage". It held that when it has been established that a prior run has economic advantages over a subsequent run, then "* * * other things being equal, the establishment of the discriminatory release system was damaging to the petitioners, who were relegated by it to a playing position inferior to that of their competitors." (327 U. S. at p. 260)

In this case it was not established that during the "first damage period" a prior run would have been an economic advantage to plaintiff. On the contrary, it appeared that during that period the character of plaintiff's theatre and the terms of its lease precluded it from competing successfully for first run pictures with the established first run theatres in Milwaukee (R. 809, 811).

In addition, the proof here did not establish that any "system", or any acts by defendants, relegated plaintiff to second run. On the contrary, it established that the second run policy under which plaintiff exhibited pictures at that time was exactly what it wanted and asked for (R. 377-78, 465).

IT WAS WITHIN THE AUTHORITY OF THE COURT BELOW, UNDER RULE 52(a), F. R. C. P., TO SET ASIDE THE FINDING OF THE TRIAL COURT THAT PLAINTIFF DEMANDED FIRST RUN PICTURES IN 1946 AND, IN SO DOING, IT DID NOT COME IN CONFLICT WITH *UNITED STATES* v. *YELLOW CAB CO.*

Plaintiff's petition (p. 8) makes, but does not argue, the assertion that the court below had no right to set aside the finding of the trial court that plaintiff made oral demands for first run pictures in 1946. That a reviewing court has that right, under Rule 52(a), when on the entire evidence it is left with a "definite and firm conviction" that a mistake has been made, was the ruling of this Court in *United States* v. *Gypsum Co.*, 1948, 333 U. S. 364, 395. To the same effect are the decisions of several Courts of Appeal.*

The case cited by plaintiff, *United States* v. *Yellow Cab Co.*, 1949, 338 U. S. 338, does not hold otherwise. It holds merely that this Court will not grant what virtually amounts to a trial *de novo* by reviewing the entire record from which a trial court has drawn permissible inferences of intent, motive and desire. In so holding, this Court said that "* * * of course, it would be our duty to correct clear error, even in findings of fact * * *" (p. 342).

The opinion below, taken as a whole, shows very clearly that the Court of Appeals was not disposed to set aside lightly anything which the trial court had found. It must have felt, therefore, as it had every reason to feel, a "definite and firm conviction" that the trial court had made a serious mistake in believing that plaintiff demanded first run pictures in 1946.

Even if the court below had been wrong in setting aside that finding of the trial court, its error still would not have been cause for reversal because the fact still would remain that plaintiff, prior to December 26, 1946, did not have a theatre suitable for the exhibition of pictures on first run, so that, in any event, the court below was correct in setting aside the award of damages for the "first damage period."

---

*For example:

> *Chatz* v. *Armour Plant Employees' Credit Union*, 7 Cir. 1946, 154 F. 2d 236, 239, cert. den. 1946, 329 U. S. 728;
>
> *Aetna Life Ins. Co.* v. *Kepler*, 8 Cir. 1941, 116 F. 2d 1, 4;
>
> *State Farm Mut. Automobile Ins. Co.* v. *Bonacci*, 8 Cir. 1940, 111 F. 2d 412, 415;
>
> *Special Service Co.* v. *Delaney*, 5 Cir. 1949, 172 F. 2d 16, 19;
>
> *Lassiter* v. *Guy F. Atkinson Co.*, 9 Cir. 1949, 176 F. 2d 984, 993.

THE COURT BELOW HAD STRONG AND VALID REASONS, NOT INDICATIVE OF ANY DESIRE TO UNDERMINE THE ANTITRUST LAWS, FOR REDUCING THE AWARD OF ATTORNEY'S FEES AND STRIKING FROM THE DECREE THE "BAN ON CROSS-LICENSING".

The $225,000 attorney's fee awarded plaintiff by the trial court would have compensated plaintiff's chief counsel and his two young assistants, whose time was approximately one-half of all devoted to plaintiff's case (R. 3393) and whose salaries were under $400 per month (R. 3399), at the rate of $95.00 per hour for each of them. The fee allowed was well over 50% of the damages claimed and recovered by the plaintiff, before trebling.

Experienced trial attorneys, competent to handle major trial work, can be employed in Chicago for $200 per day (R. 3404, 3417).

The court below felt strongly that the award of attorney's fees was excessive. It is submitted that the facts confirm that opinion more strongly than could any argument by defendants.

The trial court's decree prohibited any of the defendant distributors from licensing pictures to so-called "deluxe" neighborhood theatres in Milwaukee operated by affiliates of defendant distributors (R. 3628-29). Such "deluxe" theatres played pictures on second run.

Plaintiff never has pretended otherwise than that this so-called "ban on cross-licensing" was in effect and intent a decree of divestiture, since the "deluxe" theatres could not be operated by the affiliated exhibitors or anyone else without the pictures which the decree would have denied them (R. 3515-16, 3613). Plaintiff cannot demonstrate that such a divestiture would be of any future benefit or protection to it. Other provisions in the decree have secured to the plaintiff its desired right to obtain films for exhibition on first run. The enjoyment of that right will be in no way prejudiced or threatened by the continued operation of second run theatres by exhibitors which now are affiliated with defendant distributors.

The required divestiture by the affiliates of defendants of their "deluxe" theatres would be heavily punitive as to them. In addition, such a divestiture would disregard, and possibly do great violence to, the rights of the owners of those theatres, not affiliated with defendants in any way, who presumably leased them to the affiliated exhibitors in preference to any other use which they could make of their property.

That the court below did not lightly undertake to change any provision of the trial court's decree is attested by the statement in its opinion that it recognized that "the trial court is endowed with a wide discretion in formulating a decree to meet the situation before it" and that it decided to approve a number of provisions in the decree written by plaintiff's council even though it considered them to be of "doubtful propriety" (R. 3766).

CONCLUSION

Defendant respondents respectfully submit that the plaintiff's petition for a writ of certiorari should not be granted. The grounds presented are without merit.

MILES G. SEELEY
EDWARD R. JOHNSTON
JOHN F. CASKEY
VINCENT O'BRIEN
Attorneys for the Respondents.

December 18, 1951.

IN THE

Supreme Court of the United States

OCTOBER TERM, 1951.

No. 439

MILWAUKEE TOWNE CORPORATION, A CORPORATION,
Petitioner,

vs.

L O E W'S INCORPORATED, A CORPORATION; PARA-
MOUNT PICTURES, INC., A CORPORATION; RKO RADIO
PICTURES, INC., A CORPORATION; TWENTIETH CEN-
TURY-FOX FILM CORPORATION, A CORPORATION;
WARNER BROS. PICTURES DISTRIBUTING COR-
PORATION, A CORPORATION; WARNER BROS. CIR-
CUIT MANAGEMENT CORPORATION, A CORPORA-
TION; WARNER BROS. THEATRES, INC., A CORPORA-
TION; AND COLUMBIA PICTURES CORPORATION,
A CORPORATION,

Respondents.

REPLY TO RESPONDENTS' ANSWER TO PETITION FOR CERTIORARI.

THOMAS C. McCONNELL,
Attorney for Petitioner.

THE GUNTHORP-WARREN PRINTING COMPANY,ı

INDEX.

CITATIONS.

CASES.

STATUTES AND MISCELLANEOUS.

No. 439.

MILWAUKEE TOWNE CORPORATION, A CORPORATION,

Petitioner,

vs.

L O E W'S INCORPORATED, A CORPORATION; P A R A-
MOUNT PICTURES, INC., A CORPORATION; RKO RADIO
PICTURES, INC., A CORPORATION; TWENTIETH CEN-
TURY-FOX FILM CORPORATION, A CORPORATION;
WARNER BROS. PICTURES DISTRIBUTING COR-
PORATION, A CORPORATION; WARNER BROS. CIR-
CUIT MANAGEMENT CORPORATION, A CORPORA-
TION; WARNER BROS. THEATRES, INC., A CORPORA-
TION; AND COLUMBIA PICTURES CORPORATION,
A CORPORATION,

Respondents.

REPLY TO RESPONDENTS' ANSWER TO PETITION FOR CERTIORARI.

I.

**THE DECISION OF THE COURT OF APPEALS THAT A DEMAND
THE ACCEPTANCE OF WHICH IS PRECLUDED BY CON-
SPIRACY IS A CONDITION PRECEDENT TO BRINGING A
CIVIL ANTI-TRUST SUIT RAISES A QUESTION OF PARA-
MOUNT PUBLIC IMPORTANCE IN THE ADMINISTRATION OF
THE ANTI-TRUST LAWS.**

While respondents make a strenuous effort to persuade
this Court (pages 3-11 of the answer) that the Court of
Appeals did not set aside the award of damages for the

"first damage period" upon the ground that "plaintiff made no demand during that period for pictures to exhibit on first run", the opinion itself conclusively demonstrates the contrary. The Court of Appeals said (R. 3761) "We are of the view that it cannot be held that defendants' conspiracy was the direct and proximate cause of plaintiff's damage because it was prevented from negotiating and obtaining first run pictures *in the absence of a demand or request*". (Italics ours.) It hardly lies in the mouths of respondents to assign some other view to the Court and the fact that they attempt it is a tacit admission, that the Court's view cannot be sustained.

This ruling reversed the finding of the trial court (Finding 56, R. 3343) holding:

> "56. Plaintiff has been damaged by the uniform zoning and clearance schedule adopted and used by defendants by virtue of the classification of the Miller Theatre as a second run theatre and by clearances created under said schedule and imposed and carried out by agreement between defendants during the period from May 2, 1946 to August 15, 1946, *preventing plaintiff from obtaining pictures free from such restraint;* that the delay in obtaining pictures caused by such illegal classification or clearance enabled defendants to obtain patronage at their respective theatres which in the absence of such classification or clearance would have been obtained by plaintiff; that a fair measure of this damage to plaintiff's business is the difference between its box-office receipts during the period from May 2, 1946 to August 15, 1946, and the box-office receipts of Fox-Wisconsin Amusement Company in its Wisconsin Theatre during the same period, which difference, after proper adjustments for film rental and advertising, amounts to the sum of $118,101.32." (Italics ours.)

The ruling of the Court of Appeals also reversed Conclusion 9 of the trial court (R. 3347) holding:

> "9. In the instant case, the fixing of first run clear-

ance by conspiracy between defendants is not an activity normally adopted to secure pecuniary reward for the monopoly granted by the copyright laws. Here the licenses are but part of a general plan to suppress competition, for which a copyright can no more be used than can a patent; namely, a plan to deter competition between rivals in the exploitation of their licenses and, as shown by the findings, the clearances here acquired a fixed and uniform character and were made applicable to situations without regard to the special circumstances which are necessary to sustain them as reasonable restraints of trade. Further, when used, as here, as implements in a price-fixing conspiracy which was illegal *per se,* the copyrights themselves can not be used to justify the restraints on competition occasioned by the clearance. *Since plaintiff, even when operating a second run theatre, was prevented from obtaining pictures at an earlier date by such illegal clearance,* the inevitable result of the clearance was to give to defendants' theatres patronage which otherwise would have gone to plaintiff's theatre, and plaintiff was therefore necessarily damaged by the imposition of this illegal clearance during the period from May 2, 1946 to August 15, 1946.'' (Italics ours.)

The trial court further held that the only condition precedent to an action of this kind was the ownership of an "available theatre" (R. 3345). That this ruling is correct is shown by the opinion in the case of *William Goldman Theatres, Inc.* v. *Loew's, Inc., et al.,* 150 F. 2d 738, 744, where the Court said:

"* * * a course of conduct, by those who own all of the other available theatres in that area, and those who distribute the product, which eliminates from competition *the owner of the available theatre,* constitutes a violation of the statute.'' (Italics ours.)

The record shows that petitioner had an "available theatre" because its theatre was a first run theatre prior to the time that respondent Fox acquired it by lease (R. 373) and the respondent Fox, pursuant to the conspiracy and pursuant to agreements with its lessors of its Palace and Wisconsin Theatres (R. 258, 265, 352, 355) placed the theatre in a subservient position under the Milwaukee Plan (R. 247). The Miller Theatre (later renamed the Towne Theatre) posed a threat to respondents' first run monopoly (R. 223) and for this reason was held back in its playing position by the Milwaukee Plan (R. 268, 269). The theatre had an excellent location within 100 feet of Third and Wisconsin Avenues, the businest corner in Milwaukee (R. 1588, 1702, 388, 358, 1699, 1700). In the opinion of a respondent's witness Raftery, it had a better location than any other theatre in Milwaukee (R. 830). All respondents considered it a fit theatre in which to exhibit their best pictures second run (Pl. Ex. 86, R. 2373). It was obviously fit for first run exhibition if it could have obtained the pictures because it had the same location it now has and more seats (R. 522, 530). *The respondents requested a finding that prior to December 26, 1946, petitioner's theatre was unsuitable for the exhibition of first run pictures* (R. 3361). *It was refused by the trial court* (R. 3624).

The fact that $200,000.00 was spent in making it the best theatre in Milwaukee, did not militate against an earlier playing position before such remodeling. This is shown by the fact that the Strand Theatre, operated by the respondent Fox, played first run pictures on a moveover run (R. 337) prior to the time it remodeled its theatre (R. 1769, 1782) and there is no reason suggested why petitioner's theatre, could not have done likewise if it had obtained the pictures. It is true that petitioner's theatre was not available for the playing of first run pictures when it was closed for remodeling, but no claim was made for damages during that period.

The fact that a demand was futile is adjudicated by the Court of Appeals, as follows (R. 3755):

> "Briefly, the record discloses that defendants or their predecessors in 1930 formulated a plan which was revised in 1933, known as the Milwaukee Plan. That this plan amounted to a conspiracy in violation of the anti-trust laws is not seriously disputed. It is plain that under this plan certain theatres, some of which were owned and operated by the defendants, were awarded a first run position for the exhibition of films with certain designated periods of clearances, and that others were awarded a second run position, also with certain designated periods of clearances over subsequent runs. *It is shown that the theatre subsequently acquired by plaintiff was designated as a second run theatre, and we think it is reasonable to conclude, as the court found, that it continued to occupy such a position after it was acquired by the plaintiff.*" (Italics ours.)

The entire contention made in respondents' answer (pages 3-11) that petitioner's theatre was unsuitable is beside the point. The competitive forces that in an open market would have determined its "suitability" were precluded by respondents' conspiracy. Since respondents were unwilling to let petitioner compete for first run pictures it certainly does not lie in their mouths to now say such competition would have been unavailing because petitioner's theatre was "unsuitable." Further, the suitability of petitioner's theatre is irrelevant to the question raised here as to whether the Court of Appeals has adversely affected the administration of the anti-trust laws by a ruling without equivocation that "a person aggrieved by the deprivation of a right either statutory or constitutional" cannot "recover for such deprivation *in the absence of a demand or request for its exercise.*" This ruling is made in the face of the finding by the Court of Appeals itself that the respondents' conspiracy assigned petitioner's theatre to a second run playing position (R. 3755) and the further finding that even after spending $200,000.00 remodeling the theatre and making written demands for first run pictures, petitioner still could not get the pictures because of respondents' conspiracy (R. 3756-3758).

There is, therefore, no escape from the conclusion that the Court of Appeals has interpolated into the anti-trust laws the requirement that a futile demand is a condition precedent to any action for damages occasioned by a conspiracy and monopoly held to be illegal under those laws. This, we submit, raises a question of great importance in the administration of these laws.

The decision of the issue set forth in the opinion of the Court of Appeals is obviously wrong and designed to work untold harm in future civil anti-trust litigation. The true rule is stated with clarity in the case of *Ulrich, et al.* v. *Ethyl Gasoline Corporation*, 2 Federal Rules Decisions, 357, 359:

> "The plaintiffs claim damages from October 19, 1936, up to the date of filing of the petition on August 5, 1940. The defendant contends that proof of damage should be limited to the period between June 30, 1938, when the plaintiff's request for a license was refused and December 22, 1938, when they began to get a regular supply of Ethyl gasoline from the Kentucky Consumers Coil Company. I believe that the defendant's view on this question is much too narrow. If the defendant is guilty of an unlawful monopoly the plaintiff could be damaged by reason thereof before he actually applied for a license. *The refusal of his application was a confirmation of facts which may have existed for a considerable period of time prior thereto.*" (Italics ours.)

At pages 7 and 8 of the answer the further contention is made that petitioner did not want first run pictures during the first damage period. There is nothing in the record to sustain such a position except the request which was made for second run pictures, which the trial court found was made only after first run pictures had been refused and in order to keep petitioner's theatre open (R. 3338). Further, the record conclusively established by the testimony of Edward C. Raftery, a respondent's witness, that Spheeris and Papas were seeking to license first run pictures for the Miller Theatre as early as April, 1946 (R. 807). Raftery was questioned on this subject on cross-examination as follows: ·

Q.   Were they talking to you about second and third run United Artists pictures?

A.   Of course not (R. 826).

When he was further questioned on first run pictures Raftery's answer was unequivocal that the main thing that petitioner was interested in was first run pictures in April of 1946 (R. 822). It was, therefore, conclusively established that petitioner was seeking first run pictures from United Artists, and respondents' counsel conceded in the Court below that if petitioner's theatre "was going to be a first run theatre, it wanted first run pictures from everybody, not just from somebody, not just for some days of the week" (R. 1965). While it is obviously impossible to reargue the facts contained in a three thousand page record in a petition for certiorari, there is no question but that on this record there is substantial evidence in support of the trial court's findings (R. 3341) that petitioner was prevented from obtaining first run pictures by the defendants' conspiracy. This constitutes the so-called "fact of damage" as a matter of law and the decision of this Court in *Bigelow, et al.* v. *RKO Radio Pictures, Inc., et al.*, 327 U. S. 251, so holds.

II.

IT WAS NOT WITHIN THE AUTHORITY OF THE COURT BELOW TO SET ASIDE THE FINDINGS OF THE TRIAL COURT THAT PETITIONER HAD DEMANDED FIRST RUN PICTURES IN 1946, AND THE DECISION OF THE COURT BELOW IS IN CONFLICT WITH THAT OF THIS COURT IN THE CASE OF UNITED STATES vs. YELLOW CAB COMPANY.

Under Rule 52(a), findings of fact entered by a trial court cannot be set aside by a reviewing court unless "clearly erroneous".

The trial court held (Findings 34 and 35, R. 3338):

"34. Sometime between April 3, 1946 and April 18, 1946, plaintiff sought to license first run pictures from all defendant distributors and orally demanded that it be permitted so to do from the Branch Managers of said companies; that plaintiff thereupon was advised that the Miller Theatre was not entitled to license first run pictures because it was a second-run theatre and the pictures were being sold first run to the Fox theatres and the Warner theatres.

"35. While negotiations for first run pictures continued with United Artists, plaintiff, in order to keep its theatre open, requested and obtained pictures second run."

These findings were entered because the senior judge of the District Court believed the testimony of Spheeris (R. 369, 370, 371, 372-375, 380-381, 466) that such demands were made.

The trial court characterized the opposing testimony of respondents' witnesses (R. 3566) as follows:

The Court: "Now, I observed these men who testified here. They are bright, shrewd men. But their loyalty to somebody away, away off yonder far transcends their fear of this or any other court, or, I am sure, their fear of the hereafter. That is the situation."

In the case of *United States* v. *Yellow Cab Company*, 338 U. S. 338, 342, this Court said:

> "* * * Such a choice between two permissible views of the weight of the evidence is not 'clearly erroneous.' "

This Court further said at page 341 of that opinion:

> "Findings as to the design, motive and intent with which men act depend peculiarly upon the credit given to witnesses by those who see and hear them. If defendants' witnesses spoke the truth, the findings are admittedly justified."

In the instant case, the reason for the rule becomes abundantly clear by the unconscionable result achieved by the decision of the Court of Appeals. Here Andrew M. Spheeris, a graduate of the University of Wisconsin and of its Law School (R. 362) and a Lieutenant Colonel in the United States Army (R. 363), who served his country in World War II with General Patton's Army in the European theatre of operations (R. 537), is condemned a perjurer by a court who never saw him, on controverting testimony that the trial judge held came from the mouths of perjurers (R. 3566).

It is interesting to compare the decision of the Court of Appeals for the Third Circuit in the recent case of *Milgram, et al.* v. *Loew's, Inc., et al.*, C. C. H. Tr. Reg. Rep. Par. 62,938 (C. A. 3, 1951) where the court said:

> "But we cannot stress too strongly that the credibility of those witnesses was a matter peculiarly within the province of the trial judge. Rule 52, Federal Rules of Civil Procedure. * * * It may be noted that there was a conflict between the testimony of Milgram and that of the many district managers and salesmen with respect to Milgram's alleged requests for first run features. Milgram had testified concerning conversations which the distributors' witnesses in many cases denied.

As the trial judge concluded that Milgram's testimony was more accurate, it is implicit that the credibility of defendants' witnesses was damaged in his eyes.''

We submit that if the present decision stands, little if anything remains of Rule 52(a) of the Federal Rules of Civil Procedure, and this Court's ruling in the *Yellow Cab Company* case that a trial court's determination of which witness to believe cannot be held "clearly erroneous" is in effect reversed.

CONCLUSION.

As we have pointed out, the questions involved in this petition are of importance to the public and to the administration of the anti-trust laws and transcend the rights of these litigants. The real question presented is whether or not the Court of Appeals for the Seventh Circuit is to be permitted to destroy the efficacy of the anti-trust laws in that Circuit by legal interpolations which have no justification in the law or in the statutes. The harm to the public interest is created by the establishment in the instant case of a precedent which if permitted to stand will destroy the rights of many victims of anti-trust violations in subsequent litigation under those laws.

For the reasons given here and in the petition, we submit that a writ of certiorari should issue, limited to the issues raised in the petition.

Respectfully submitted,

THOMAS C. McCONNELL,
Attorney for Petitioner.

Lightning Source UK Ltd.
Milton Keynes UK
UKHW05f0930260718
326318UK00006B/385/P